25.27

D0819511

Igloo

Written by

Yasmine A. Cordoba

Illustrated by

Kimberly L. Dawson Kurnizki

The Rourke Book Company, Inc.
Vero Beach, Florida 32964

Printed in the United States of America

Library of Congress Cataloging-in-Publication Data

Cordoba, Yasmine A., 1970-
 Igloo / Yasmine A. Cordoba.
    p. cm. — (Native American homes)
 Includes bibliographical references and index.
 Summary: Explains how climate and the nomadic culture influenced the Arctic peoples in their choice of dwellings. Includes directions for making a model igloo.
 ISBN 1-55916-277-5
 1. Igloos—Juvenile literature. 2. Inuit—Dwellings—Juvenile literature. [1. Igloos. 2. Inuit—Dwellings. 3. Arctic peoples.] I. Title. II. Series.

E99 .E7 C67 2000
971.9004'9712—dc21

                                                                    00–038721

Contents

The Arctic

The Arctic sits at the top of the Earth with the North Pole in the middle. It contains parts of many countries, including Canada, Greenland, and the United States. The Arctic ends and the Subarctic begins where the trees stop growing; it is too cold in the Arctic for trees to grow.

Arctic winters are long and severe, lasting nine to eleven months. Large areas of the sea and land freeze. Winds and dangerous storms cut across endless miles of snow. Winter days are short, and the nights are long. In the most northern parts of the Arctic it is dark for weeks at a time. As summer nears, daylight lasts longer.

The plants and animals of the Arctic change with the seasons. In the winter, there are no plants. Many animals move south, but seals, whales, and walruses remain in the frigid ocean. By summer and fall (roughly August and September), some snow melts and the top layer of the ground defrosts. Mosses, grasses, and even shrubs grow. *Migratory* animals appear, such as musk oxen, caribou, salmon, ducks, and geese.

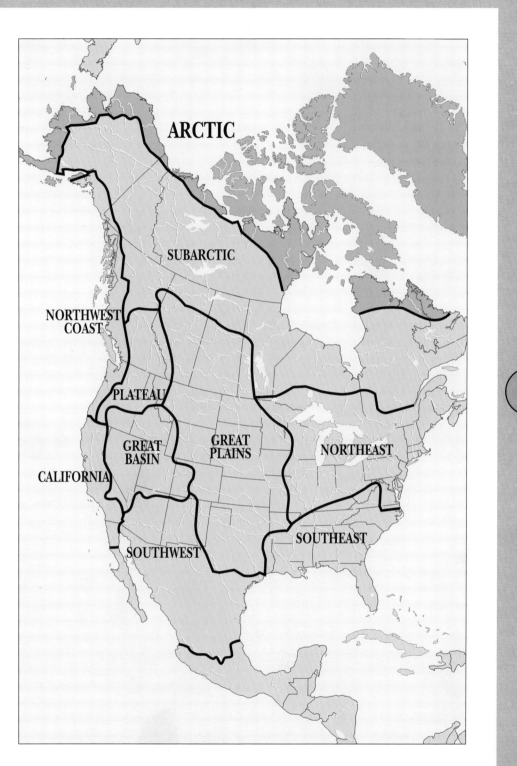

ARCTIC

SUBARCTIC

NORTHWEST
COAST

PLATEAU

GREAT
BASIN

GREAT
PLAINS

NORTHEAST

CALIFORNIA

SOUTHWEST

SOUTHEAST

5

Arctic People

The people who first settled the Arctic regions came from Asia about 3,000 years ago. Aleutian, Greenlandic, Inuktitut, and Yupik are a few of the languages they speak. Natives of the Arctic call themselves by many different names, such as Inuit, Alutiit, and Yupik. All of them mean "the real people." The Arctic people of Alaska prefer to be called Eskimos, whereas those of Canada and Greenland usually prefer to be called Inuit.

A group of Arctic women and children gathered in a community igloo for songs and storytelling.

Arctic settlers developed special skills and knowledge that helped them to survive the harsh climate of the land. Animals provided the Arctic dwellers with many of life's necessities: meat and fat for food, furs and hides for clothing, bones and teeth for tools, *intestines* for bags and straps. The Arctic people rarely stayed in one place for long. They followed the best hunting, moving many times a year. They traveled as a single family, or sometimes in small groups. Some built dwellings that were quick and easy and could be left behind or carried away. Other houses were more *permanent* but would be abandoned for parts of the year.

Igloos

Igloos were the winter homes for the Central Inuits of northern Canada and Greenland. To survive in the Arctic, the Inuits learned to make the most of everything they had. One thing they had a lot of was snow. They used the snow to build houses called igloos. The word "igloo" comes from the Inuit word for house, *igdlu*. Native people in other parts of the Arctic used igloos only for temporary shelter while on hunting trips. Others did not use igloos at all. For centuries, the Central Inuits used them during the winter months, from around October through May.

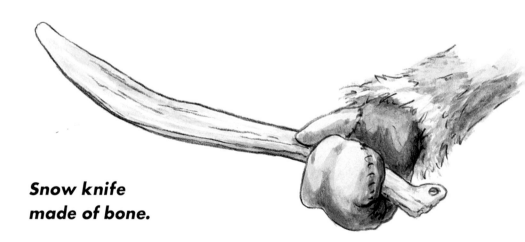

Snow knife made of bone.

A modern, temporary igloo built on the Arctic snow fields.

An igloo is built with blocks of dense snow. It is shaped like the small end of an egg. An experienced builder could make a small, temporary igloo in about an hour. Larger igloos, built to last longer, took more time and more people to build. For a family igloo, domes could be connected to make separate sleeping, working, and storage spaces. Inuits generally lived in an igloo for about a month before moving to find better hunting. A new igloo would be built at the next site.

Sometimes many families would return to the same place every year to share information, trade goods, go on group hunts, and perform ceremonies. In these settlements many igloos could be connected by tunnels or adjoining walls, so people could visit without going outside. Large, community igloos might also be built in settlements for ceremonies and dancing.

Igloos were also used for hunting. Special small igloos were used to catch birds. A hunter built an igloo around himself, just big enough to crouch inside. The igloo had a hole in the roof. Bait was placed next to the hole. When the bird landed to eat the food, the hunter grabbed its legs through the hole. Inuit hunters also built small igloos for shelter while out on overnight hunting trips.

Building an Igloo

Usually, at least two people worked together to build an igloo. One worked from the inside and one from the outside.

A 30-pound snow block is lifted into place.

Firm, evenly packed snow worked best for building igloos. Inuits used a straight, thin piece of bone, wood, or antler to test the snow. When they found good igloo snow, they used a snow knife made from a caribou antler or ivory to cut rectangular blocks. The blocks were about 2 to 3 feet (0.6 to 0.9 meter) long, 1 to 2 feet (0.3 to 0.6 meter) tall, and 4 to 6 inches (10 to 15 centimeters) thick. Each weighed up to 40 pounds (18 kilograms).

The builders placed the blocks in a circle, end to end. The snow blocks at the base of the igloo were cut at an angle so that their tops sloped upward. They were also tilted toward the center of the circle. When more blocks were placed on these blocks, they formed a spiral. The igloo was built up like a circular staircase, but it also leaned inward to create a dome.

Blocks were stacked on one another until the last block was placed at the top of the igloo. The Inuit working inside the igloo then cut a small hole in the top to make a chimney. He might also cut a hole in the side of the igloo to make a window. This hole would be filled with a clear piece of freshwater ice or a piece of animal intestine.

Shaving the blocks is important for a good fit.

Finally, the Inuit inside cut a door and crawled out of the igloo. Sometimes a porch was attached to the igloo. The builder dug a *trench* leading away from the door. Then he enclosed the trench with snow blocks in the same way as the igloo. The floor of the entry passage was dug lower than the floor of the igloo to trap cold air.

To make the igloo stronger, the builders pressed snow into the gaps between the snow blocks and smoothed the dome.

How Igloos Work

How can snow keep you warm? Blocks made from snow that is pressed tightly together have few holes or cracks in them. Air cannot easily pass through these blocks. They keep heat from people's bodies and heat from oil lamps inside, and they keep cold air outside. In this way the igloo works like a blanket. A blanket does not make heat. It keeps the heat from your body close to you and cold air from outside away from you.

In some igloos, the Inuit built a large fire inside the igloo to melt the walls. When the fire was put out, the snow would freeze again, making a strong, hard shell. No little holes were left through which warm air might escape. Sometimes Inuits hung furs along the inside of the igloo. These also helped keep the warm air inside. The temperature inside an igloo was about 65 degrees Fahrenheit (18 degrees Celsius) warmer than the temperature outside.

Inuits also knew that hot air rises and that cold air is heavier and falls. That is why the doorways of igloos were built below the level of the floor. The passage leading to the door often sloped down, away from the igloo. Cold air from outside would stay low and not rise up the passage and into the room. Warm air from inside would not move down through the door and passage and out of the igloo.

The dome-like shape of the igloo's walls made them very strong. The top of the igloo was more cone-shaped to give extra support to the roof. Igloos could resist the worst Arctic winds and storms. A grown man could stand on the top of an igloo without damaging it.

19

Living in Igloos

Inside the igloo, Inuits slept, cooked, and worked on snow platforms 3 feet (0.9 meter) high. These platforms could fill more than half the igloo. The sleeping area was at the back of the igloo, opposite the door. It was covered with moss and furs. The family slept without clothes and under fur blankets. They used their clothes for pillows. An oil lamp was placed on a platform to the side of the door. It provided light and heat. Food was cooked over the lamp, and clothes were dried by it.

During the summer, children played outside most of the time. The men were out hunting and fishing. During the winter, darkness and storms could keep everybody inside for days. Inside the igloos, the Inuits sewed and carved, told stories, sang, and danced.

Inuits sometimes formed villages. A village could be made up of as few as 30 people or as many as 500 people. The plan of a village was different every time it was built. Like an igloo, a settlement could be as small and simple or as big and complex as needed. Villages broke up when the land could no longer support them.

Other Winter Homes

In many areas of the Arctic, people did not live in igloos. *Sod-houses* and *quarmangs* were two other types of winter dwellings. They were built partially underground with frames of bones or driftwood. These homes trapped heat in the same way as igloos.

Quarmangs, or quarmaks, were dug out of the side of a hill. A tunnel led upward to the main dwelling space. The floors and walls were lined with stones or bones. The roof was made of animal skins stretched over whalebone or wooden poles. A layer of brush was added, then another layer of skins. Finally, a layer of snow covered everything. These many layers kept the quarmang warm.

Sod-houses took much time and work to build, so one sod-house was often made for several families. The house and the tunnel leading to it were dug out of the side of a hill. Wood was used to cover the floor and walls. Wood or bone poles in the corners supported the *sod* roof. Inside, each family had its own living space, and all the families shared a central area.

Summer Homes

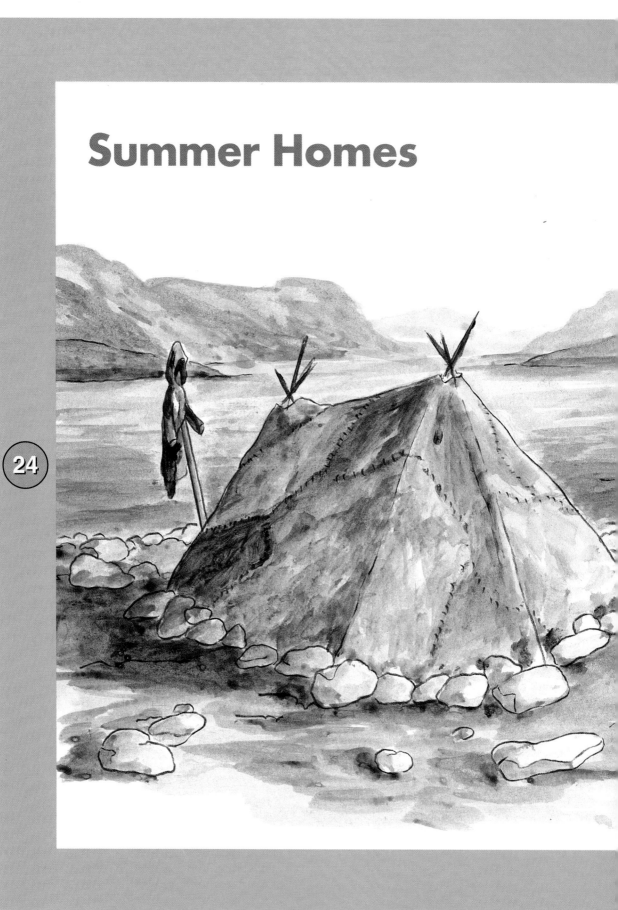

During the summer igloos, quarmangs, and sod-houses were abandoned and people moved into tents. There were several different types of tents, but all used poles of wood, bone, or straightened antlers for support and animal skins for cover. Usually the sleeping area was at the back of the tents, and fires were built outside.

One type of tent was circular, like a tipi, but needed only one pole. The pole stood in the middle with strips of seal skin attached to the top of it. These strips were stretched to the ground in a circle and held in place by stones. This cone-shaped frame was covered by seal or caribou skins.

Rectangular tents were also used in the Arctic. To build one of these, two sets of poles were crossed at their tops, creating two triangles. These triangles were the front and back of the tent and were held in place by stones. Another pole or strip of animal skin ran from the top of one triangle to the top of the other. Animal skins were stretched over this frame and held down by stones.

Arctic People Today

The people of the Arctic no longer use igloos for winter housing. They now live in modern buildings. These buildings are more permanent. They do not need to hunt as much as they once did, so they do not have to move from place to place as often. When they do hunt, Arctic people now use rifles instead of spears or bows and arrows. They fish from motorboats instead of kayaks. Snowmobiles have replaced dogsleds. They now buy or trade for clothing, tools, and food, rather than making these things.

The Arctic people no longer rely on hunting for food and tools, but they continue to hunt for furs to sell or trade. Igloos are still sometimes used for emergency shelter or for overnight hunting trips. Life in the Arctic has changed, but many Arctic people continue to keep and teach old beliefs and knowledge. The building of igloos is part of these teachings.

A powerful lantern makes this modern igloo glow in the night.

Make a Model Igloo

What you will need:

paper and pencil
ruler
bowl
2 ice cube trays
3 cups plain flour
1½ cups salt
1⅓ cups water

To make your igloo:

1. Mix 3 cups of flour, 1½ cups of salt, and half of the water in a bowl. Gradually add the remaining water. Knead until ingredients form one ball of dough.

2. Press dough into the ice cube trays to form blocks. Freeze at least 2 hours. Remove blocks. Fill 1½ trays to make about 22 blocks.

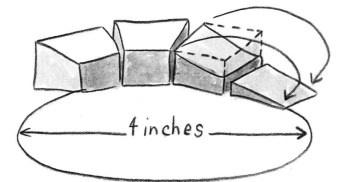

4 inches

3. On a piece of paper draw or trace a circle 4 inches (10.2 centimeters) across. Fit the blocks on their sides along the circle with the small ends facing inward. Use ruler to cut the top of the first block at a slant, and flip the top piece over to form a ramp as shown in the illustration. Continue to place blocks around the circle and up the ramp in a spiral shape. Trim blocks to fit as they close in to form a dome.

4. When the dome is finished, use trimmings to fill or chink the gaps. Carefully cut a door at the base of the igloo.

5. You can bake your igloo at 125 degrees Fahrenheit (50 degrees Celsius) until the dough is completely hard.

Glossary

caribou: an Arctic deer.

intestines: mucous-membrane-lined tube of the digestive system.

migratory: moving from one place to another or from one climate to another.

musk oxen: a large, shaggy, horned mammal of northern Canada and Greenland.

permanent: fixed and lasting.

quarmang/quarmak: a home built into the side of a hill, with a foundation and walls of stone or bone and a roof made of animal skins stretched over bone or wood.

sod: grass-covered surface soil held together by tangled roots.

sod-house: a home built partially underground, with a frame of wooden poles and a roof of brush, earth, and sod.

trench: a long, narrow ditch.

Further Reading

Hiscock, Bruce. *Tundra: The Arctic Land.* New York: Atheneum, 1986.

Purdy, Susan, and Cass R. Sandak. *Eskimos: A Civilization Project Book.* New York: Franklin Watts, 1982.

Shemie, Bonnie. *Houses of Snow, Skin, and Bones.* New York: Tundra Books of Northern New York, 1989.

Steltzer, Ulli. *Building an Igloo.* New York: Henry Holt and Company, Inc, 1981.

Weiss, Harvey. *Shelters: From Tepee to Igloo.* New York: Thomas E. Crowell, 1988.

Yue, Charlotte, and David Yue. *The Igloo.* Boston: Houghton Mifflin Company, 1988.

Suggested Web Sites

Arctic Studies Center
<www.mnh.si.edu/arctic/html/features.htm>
Prince of Wales Northern Heritage Centre
Igloo—the Traditional Arctic Snow Dome
<indy4.fdl.cc.mn.us/~isk/maps/houses/ igloo.html#buttons>
Igloo Builders Guide
<home.sol.no/~gedra/igloo_bg.htm>
Search Engine Source
<www/yahooligans.com>

Index

Photo credits: Cover, p. 6, Douglas E. Wilkinson/NWT Archives; pp. 8, 13, 14, Northwest Territories, Dept. of Information/NWT Archives; p. 27, R.C. Knights/NWT Archives.